F^7: *Faith to the Seventh Power*

Building the Principles to live in Your Complete Power

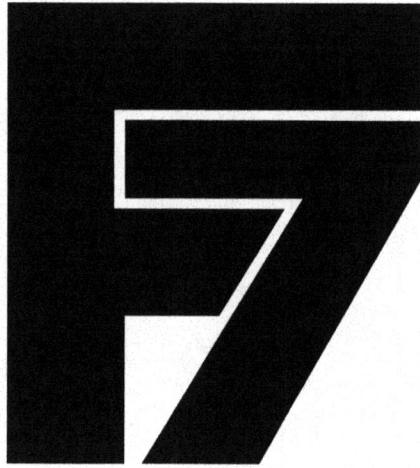

F^7: *Faith to the Seventh Power*

By Shanae Godley

2016

Unless otherwise indicated, Scripture taken from The Message. Copyright © 1993, 1994, 1995, 1996, 2000, 2001, 2002. Used by permission of NavPress Publishing Group.

THE HOLY BIBLE, NEW INTERNATIONAL VERSION®, NIV® Copyright © 1973, 1978, 1984, 2011 by Biblica, Inc.® Used by permission. All rights reserved worldwide.

First Printing: January 2016

ISBN: 978-1-329-82490-4

Editorial Assistance by: Kimberly Lucas, Hereamii, LLC
Hereamii.com@gmail.com

Ordering Information:
Special discounts are available on quantity purchases by corporations, associations, educators, and others. For details, contact the publisher at beopoulentbydesign@gmail.com.

www.ShanaeGodley.com

www.lulu.com

Dedication

In loving memory of...

Grandma Boot,
An amazing woman of faith

Thank you for showing me what it looks like to stand in faith. You believed in me and loved me, when I couldn't do it for myself. You are appreciated and greatly missed by all.

Contents

Introduction

Faith to the Seventh Power

Raise Your Faith

Activating Power 1: Character
    There's Always Hope

Activating Power 2: Knowledge
    Groundbreaking Vision

Activating Power 3: Discipline
    Grow into Greatness

Activating Power 4: Perseverance
    Be Strong

Activating Power 5: Godliness
    My Worship is For Real

Activating Power 6: Kindness
    Giving on Purpose

Activating Power 7: Love
    Love without Limits

Powers Activated

Introduction

For all of my fellow math lovers, let's talk about exponents for a moment. If you are not a math lover, don't worry; this won't take long. Exponents, as we learned in grade school, are shorthand for repeated multiplication of the same number by itself. This number is called a "constant factor". We often refer to the use of exponents as "raising [the constant factor] to a power". For instance, 7^2 is equivalent to raising the number seven to the power of two. Just like we raise a number (or constant factor) to a power in math, we should raise our faith (our constant factor) to a power in life.

Think with me. If seven is raised to the second power (7^2), then your equation would be 7x7. Correct? Therefore, if faith is raised to the seventh power (F^7), your equation would be Faith x Faith x Faith x Faith x Faith x Faith x Faith. That is a lot of faith when it's multiplied by itself, but is that necessary? Jesus reminds us in the Bible that we only need faith the size of a mustard seed, which is really, really tiny. So, instead of multiplying faith by itself, let's try a new equation. Let's raise faith to the complete powers of God.

Did you just ask, "What powers?"

Is God not a superhero?

Well, yes. Yes, God is a superhero.

He has super powers, and He has shared them with you.

He wants your life to be amazing, but you must first embrace your powers.

In this book you will find ten chapters of life changing information. Each chapter is formatted to give you information about the powers that God has gifted to you. At the end of each chapter, take a moment to (1) Activate Your Power – through activation you can turn on the switch to building your faith. (2) Reflect on Your Power – through reflection you apply each power to your life and (3) remember a few important nuggets from the chapter and keep them fresh in your mind as you continue to build your faith to the seventh power.

Please, tie your shoe laces and run this race with me, as we raise our faith to the seventh power!

Faith to the Seventh Power

God is the ultimate superhero of our lives, but he has shared his powers with us so that we might live an opulent life. There are seven powers of God that this book will focus on: Character, Knowledge, Self-Control, Perseverance, Godliness, Kindness and Love. The Message Bible says in 2 Peter 1:8, that "no grass will grow under our feet, no day will pass without its reward, and we will mature in our experience of Jesus," if we keep these seven specific powers active and growing in our lives. When these powers build upon one another and remain active in our lives, we can finish this race and receive whatever we have the faith to run after.

It is a fact that in life, we run towards what we believe the most. Therefore, it is important to set your faith in God and run the race that has been set before you; not the race that has been set before your friends, your family or co-workers. God has given you a race that is significant and tailor-made for you. No one else can run it for you. Even your finish line is yours to reach; the accomplishments and consequences all belong to you. Thus, you cannot allow your present circumstances to disqualify you or knock you off of the tracks. It is time that you take responsibility for your race and run.

The best part of running your own race is that you can set the pace of your run. You define your success, and only you know what it takes to reach your goals. At times, there may be things in your path that block your run. Do not avoid these roadblocks; address them right away. Make sure you stop to re-adjust, but stay conscious of your environment and do not get stuck. Your path may appear blocked, but it will reopen again someday and you must be prepared to move forward.

You might ask, "How can I be prepared for a journey I've never been on?" What does this preparation look like? What if you are like me and don't like to run? What will it take to prepare for a race that can be won by faith, not by foot? These are all questions I've asked, and what I've learned along the way is that all success is goal driven – even when the race is based on my faith. I must set my mind on what means the most. I must set some goals.

Some of our goals are short in nature. These are set for the purpose of moving from one place to another in a small amount of time. For example, a short-term goal might read, "In four weeks I will lose five pounds." The run to this goal is short lived. It is possible to reach, but will require a much focused run for a short period of time. Let's call this a "sprinting-goal". These races are run swiftly and require both focused speed and agility.

Let's face it. Most of us don't run with speed. We run slowly, but for longer periods of time. Our life's race is much like that, slow and long. Therefore, we must set long-term goals; we'll call these "walking-goals". There is no doubt that the goal can be met, but it will take much patience, long-suffering, and the setting of some sprinting goals along the way. We run the race day by day, and with each stride along the tracks of life, we know that our dreams can be fulfilled. No matter how long the path, this race is important to you.

Right now, we are using running as a metaphor to represent how we are to live a life of faith, but if we take a moment to think about life there are many other metaphors we can use: growing like a plant, standing like the great oak tree, or changing from a caterpillar to a beautiful butterfly. The Bible makes it simple; we are to "walk by faith and not by sight". The fact of the matter is that regardless of the example we use, faith is still the foundation. Nothing in life can move, function, change, or grow without the belief that it can happen, and our lives are no different. Faith is the foundation. It is the constant factor in our lives.

Activate Your Power...
"Don't lose a minute in building on [the power] you have been given, complementing your basic faith with good character, spiritual understanding, alert discipline, passionate patience, reverent wonder, warm friendliness and generous love, each dimension fitting into and developing the others."
(2 Peter 1:5-7)

Reflect on Your Power...
I know you wish you had some really cool super powers, like speed or the ability to fly, but God saw fit that the powers that build upon your faith would benefit you more greatly.
How can you use these powers, that God has given you, to change the world?

_____

_____

_____

_____

_____

_____

_____

Remember these nuggets...

1. Faith is the foundation of our lives – It will always be a constant factor.

2. You must define your own success – this is your race.

3. Nothing in life can move, function, change, or grow without the belief that it can happen.

4. It is necessary to set some sprinting and some walking goals for your life.

Raise Your Faith

Twelve years ago, when I reunited with the Christian faith, I had no idea what it took to walk by faith. Beyond church songs and popular Bible verses, I had yet to find a systematic way of understanding what it would take to build capacity within myself to be the best me that God wanted me to be. Like many Christians I, too, was brainwashed to think that the acceptance of salvation was where I earned my seat in the kingdom of God. I can remember so clearly the day that I gave my life to Christ, sitting in the back of the church and feeling a tingle in my body that pricked my heart and brought down a stream of tears like I'd never experienced before. It was my very first Mother's Day, as a mom. Just as I had been teaching my daughter her ABC's (at the ripe age of two months), it was now my turn to say the ABC's of salvation. In church that day, I Accepted Christ as the lord of my life, I Believed in my heart that he died and rose again, and then I Confessed with my mouth this new found commitment of faith.

The final words of the minister who prayed with me that day still ring in my ear, "May the peace of God be with you!" Exiting the old, rugged church building with faith that had not been built was equivalent to sending a soldier out to face the cold, dark world without a gun. No one bothered to tell me that while I felt like a mighty oak tree, I was really only a seed. As my life moved on, I sheepishly quieted the voice within and figured that walking silently was much easier than running a race. Peace was nowhere to be found because my faith had not yet been developed.

Here are some things about faith that it has taken me twelve years to learn. First, faith is the most powerful tool you have in your toolbox of life. Faith can be summed up by having confidence in God and His promises – even when you don't have any proof of His existence through your five senses. I've found faith to be my driving force - the focus of my run. Because of faith, I have accomplished some pretty amazing tasks in my life including the completion of a Master's Degree, getting married, having children, traveling, and getting jobs that I wanted. Above all, learning to walk in faith has improved my relationship with God. God likes it when I trust Him more than I trust what I can see, smell, taste, touch, or hear. My faith gives Him joy and then He gives me peace and strength. It's a win-win for both of us.

Secondly, it does not take an astronomical amount of faith to touch the heart of God. The Bible says to have faith the size of a mustard seed to move mountains, not to have faith the size of a mountain to move mustard seeds. I thought I had to have lots of faith before God would hear my prayers and release His promises. In fact, often times, I would pray with the mindset of "This will never happen" or "I doubt if God even heard that prayer." What I didn't realize was that I could not have doubt and faith at the same time. I had to have faith, even if it was a small amount, but I had to believe it with all of my heart.

Finally, the promises of God are released when we build upon our faith. Since getting married and having my sons, I have learned much about superheroes. Each hero has his or her own power and that power must be strengthened and refined in order for it to be effective. Superman had to learn how to harness his strength. Spider-Man had to learn to swing from spider webs. Cyclops (a member of the X-Men) had to learn to control his laser vision so he wouldn't burn everything in sight. The same stands true for us. As we walk in faith, we must learn to harness the power within. We must learn to build upon the powers we have, to make them stronger and more refined. The best thing about all of this is that we don't just have one power. We have seven: Character, Knowledge, Self-Control, Perseverance, Godliness, Kindness, and Love. As we add these powers to our faith, we will have the ability to do wonderful things. See the chart below as a guide to building upon your faith.

If we add (and activate) these powers...	We will have these attributes...
Faith	A strong foundation in Christ
Character	Hope
Knowledge	Vision
Self-Control	Growth
Perseverance	Strength
Godliness	Connectedness
Kindness	Life
Love	Power to pursue the desires of your heart!

Activate Your Power:

Before we get too far on our journey, I want to challenge you to raise your faith to the power of God, that He might grab hold of your faith and give you the desires of your heart. Acknowledge the desires of your heart. They will give you purpose.

Reflect on Your Power:

What are your heart's desires? What are some things that you would like to happen in your life?

List a few of them here.

_____

_____

_____

_____

_____

Remember these Nuggets:

1. Salvation is as simple as **ABC** – Accept Christ as Lord of your life, Believe that he died and rose from the dead so that you could have abundant life, and Confess with your mouth the word of God.
2. Faith is the most powerful tool you have in your toolbox of life.
3. Faith can be as small as a mustard seed and still work wonders.
4. Faith does not work where there is doubt.

Power #1: Character

"There's Always Hope"

If you have ever taken a chemistry class or experimented with chemicals, then you know that experiments usually start with a base chemical. Once the base is established, other chemicals are added to observe reactions. Sometimes that reaction is small, but sometimes it produces a big "BOOM!" The chemist usually hopes for a certain reaction, but it doesn't always happen. As we experiment in life, we do the same thing. Faith is our base, and it is up to us to add things to our lives that will cause a reaction. Whether it produces a small reaction in the world or a big "BOOM!" is up to us. The more we add, the greater the reaction.

Scientists have discovered that the best chemical reaction you will ever experience will happen between your ears; it will happen in your mind. What you learn each moment is added to what you believe about the world. This new information, when added to the old, dictates your actions and reactions. It tells you which emotion should be displayed in certain situations and makes it hard for you to control your tears or anger. Even your words are subject to this control. This chemical reaction is powerful enough to change the way you speak by giving you permission to say things like "I can't help it," or "That's the way I was raised."

The fact of the matter is, what you learned as a child is impacting who you are right now. Right and wrong behaviors are learned early in life. For instance, while your parents may have taught you the meaning of hard work and achieving your goals, they may have left out how to take care of your health. They forgot to tell you that without your health, you cannot work. More importantly, they may have forgotten to teach you how to plan for mishaps and mistakes when things go wrong. And trust me; things will go wrong. But, there is hope.

It is the basic principle of cause and effect. When you believe positive things, your life is affected positively. When you believe negative things, your life is affected negatively. It amazes me how you can think someone does not like you and then spend countless hours pondering why. I did this a lot as a teen girl. Wondering, "Is it my clothes or shoes? Did I say something wrong?" Finally, you think, "They must be jealous!" and your negative self-consciousness is awakened. A negative seed of insecurity or uncertainty may have been planted in your mind, and once it grows inside of your mind it makes you more guarded, defensive, and less attentive. Ultimately, you lose trust in people. Consider this: none of this happens because of your words or actions, but from a thought. Research has proven over and over again that what you think about the most will dictate your decisions.

As simple as it may sound, it's not always understood. Try this. If you feed your mind negative messages about life, what will happen? You will think and act on negative things. You cannot consistently add negative thoughts to your mind and expect to think about positive things, right? If the music you listen to every day talks about shooting people and disrespecting women, your mind hears the words and the seed is planted as a thought. The more you hear the song, the more you start to believe it, and your heart gets connected. Eventually you will begin to believe that it's okay to call women bad names and change your values in life.

On the contrary, plant positive seeds into your mind. The simplest, yet most energetic, form of life is in the seed. Your thoughts are seeds that should produce life, not destruction. There are plenty of ways to get positive thoughts into your mind. Reading a good book, watching an inspiring movie, listening to a motivational speaker, or choosing music that builds you up instead of tearing you down are just a few. Try going to church on a Sunday Morning for no other reason than to get an uplifting message of hope. Call a friend who naturally encourages people all of the time and ask for something positive. Do whatever you have to do to get a positive message into your mind.

A positive message is like clean, refreshing water. Your brain is like a pitcher. If you pour more clean water into the pitcher, the water will remain clear and your thoughts will, too. But, if you have a pitcher of clean water and pour dirt into it, the water will become dirty. This is how the brain works. When you allow negative thoughts to enter or live in your mind they become a part of your soul and permeate your heart. Whether positive or negative, you are bound to have a reaction.

Some of these thoughts don't come because of something we did. Some of them are thoughts we learned from our past. What principles or values did you learn from your past? Did your grandmother teach you her famous recipe? What behaviors did you pick up from your parents that make you the person you are today? Do not underestimate the power your past experiences have in helping or hindering you in your current life. Face them. Embrace them. Deal with them, but do not let them cause negative reactions in your life. No matter what your past experiences are or what your parents did not tell you, even the smallest amount of faith can create something great. How you handle this greatness is called character.

When I think of the word character, I think about TV show characters or ones you read about in great books. Each character has their very own distinctive style. For instance, there's a 90s TV show with a character that I really admire. The young guy wears very colorful, baggy clothes. His hats are usually turned backwards. He's loud, yet artistic. He believes in love and family, but doesn't really care much for things that are not authentic. I've never seen a character with such an original style. I wonder if that is what people say about you. "I admire you. I've never seen a character like you, with such an original style."

Your character is your virtue. As my sister puts it – character is your "wow factor". It is the quality of life which makes you stand out as excellent. You were created in excellence; so standing out from others to show off your God-given ability to perform heroic deeds is going to have some positive reactions, including blessings, favor, and increase. However, as many of us know, character is often defined in the most negative of situations.

When I first became a mom I struggled with all kinds of issues. I was a senior in college and was due to deliver my baby the first few weeks of the year. The consequences of a one-night stand in my dorm room had now caused me to be the sickest and most depressed I had ever been. I was carrying a child that I could not care for; I could barely care for myself. I can remember stressing about how things were going to work out and praying for God to help me find an internship that would work in favor of my situation. Without completing an internship I could not graduate, and I was only months away. I had very little money, except for what I had saved from student financial aid and a part-time job I had on campus. It had become almost impossible to work, and after a while, there was no money to manage.

Through faith, a great opportunity came my way. Not only did I get an amazing internship and supervisor, I was later hired by the organization. For five months I showed up for work consistently, except for the six weeks I was allotted for maternity leave. The internship started in January; my daughter was born in February. Keep in mind, this was an unpaid internship, yet, I improved programs and established new partnerships for the organization. I put forth every effort to become an asset, even when my situation presented several liabilities to the organization. I valued hard work and dependency, and it showed in my actions. My character represented a very important value, "faith without works is dead."

Steve Maraboli puts it this way, "While intent is the seed of manifestation, action is the water that nourishes the seed." A seed of faith that has been planted in the mind (a belief or thought) must be watered before it will produce anything. Acting according to your character is the water that nourishes faith. My seed was

"Lord, I need an internship that will be flexible in my situation and be a blessing to my family." My action was - showing up, being present, and making a difference. My action was a direct reflection of my character. Can you tell what my values were?

It is critical that you know who you are and what you believe, because these things will determine your actions. When you add character to your faith, then great things will happen for you. The world you live in will make room for the genuine you: Be yourself! Faith by itself causes you to believe that greatness is coming. If it is left alone or in seed form, it will forever be left in the dark. Adding a little bit of who you are (your values and virtue) gives your seed the light it needs to have hope that it will grow into something great.

Activate Your Power:

Here's your chance to react. Give your hope permission to come alive. You have a God-given ability to perform heroic deeds and all of the qualities of life that make you stand out as excellent. Combine that with your faith and watch great things happen for you.

Reflect on Your Power:

Let's say that a company is making a movie about your life and they need to cast someone to play your role. How would you describe your character to the company so that they get the right person? This person must not only look like you, but in some ways share your characteristics and values.

Describe your character here.

_____

_____

_____

_____

_____

_____

Nuggets to Remember:

1. Faith is our base, and it is up to us to add things to our lives that will cause a positive reaction.

2. You cannot consistently add negative thoughts to your mind and expect to think about positive things.

3. What you think about the most will dictate your decisions.

4. You have the God-given ability to perform heroic deeds.

Power #2: Knowledge
"Groundbreaking Vision"

Knowledge is one of your more active super powers and should be used to impact positive change in the world. Without any effort at all, you are likely to learn something new every day. Your brain was designed to detect information and to keep it. It is up to you to get knowledge that leads you in the direction of what you believe. Knowledge sheds light and opens your mind to things you never thought possible.

As a teenager, I lived with my grandmother in a rural, country town called Tillery. There were trees and very few houses, several churches and only two stores. In essence, there was nothing to do. But I wouldn't dare tell that to my grandma. In her house, there was no such thing as "being bored", or having nothing to do. If my siblings or I ever said that we were bored or even looked bored she interpreted that to mean "you need something to do". Saying words like "I'm bored" would immediately warrant an assignment. Her theory was clear: An idle mind is the devil's workshop. So, she would give us something to do.

"Feed the chickens.

Get the eggs from the hen house.

Feed the rabbits.

Get some 'maters (tomatoes) out of the garden.

Hang the clothes on the line outside.

Mop the kitchen floor.

Learn how to cook tater jacks (my favorite desert stuffed with sweet potato, wrapped in dough, and deep fried to perfection)."

Let's just say that of all the things she asked us to do, I was not interested in any of them, not even cooking tater jacks. (I only wanted to eat them).

But that wasn't all of the tricks in her bag. Grandma understood the importance of getting knowledge, so she had the newspaper delivered to the house. She purchased encyclopedias from the door-to-door salesman who came by the house to seek payment on Saturday morning. She picked up articles and small books wherever she went and brought them home for us to read. Then, she would sit on the couch while we tell her all about the article and she listened. She would help us to understand the parts of the story that didn't seem to make any sense. One such story was in an article I read of an enslaved girl who became pregnant and was taken into the woods for an abortion procedure. An abortion that took place back then (in the 1800s), during slavery, was nothing like the abortions that take place now in doctor offices with cushioned tables and suction pipes. In fact, the gruesomeness of the story made me sad and fearful. I thought about that story for many years, and even today, I can remember the visions in my mind about the young girl and the tree she was tied to, the men who were abusing her, and the unborn child. But, I don't get sad or fearful anymore because I understand why it happened. I talked about it with Grandma; and it was through wisdom that she helped me to understand.

You see, the Bible instructs in the book of Proverbs that we should get knowledge. It is imperative that we read books and articles, and listen to instruction from teachers, leaders, and pastors. Download podcasts and audio books. Watch a movie or documentary, and seek to learn something from it. Regardless of what you do in life, allow your mind to learn. Your brain can handle more than you think. And then when you do not understand something, ask. The second part of the Bible's instruction about knowledge is to get understanding. Knowledge and understanding should go hand in hand. The message I give to my kids is this: "If you are sitting in class (at school or otherwise) and you do not understand, do not be afraid to ask for clarity." Knowledge without understanding is like kool-aid without sugar. It gives color and maybe even some flavor to your life, but the fullness of your vision will not be good without understanding. Understanding is like sugar in your kool-aid or like icing on the cake. It makes life sweeter.

What happens when we have knowledge without understanding? Let's say for a moment that I am a trusted source of information. You've known me for years and we decide to meet for lunch and to catch up on life. In the middle of our meal, I stop our conversation to tell you that your mate is cheating on you and has found love somewhere else. After you spit all of your food in my face, I presume your emotions will paint a picture in your mind of what could be happening. You begin to imagine him/her with their arms around someone else. You see them kissing or holding hands. You try to picture the "other person." Your mind gives you all of these pictures until you become angry or anxious. The knowledge you received brought visions of what could be. These types of visions can be blurry and lead you to believe things that are not true and bring about negative feelings. If you take a little time to pursue understanding, you can get to the bottom of the situation and have a clearer vision of what is actually happening. What I didn't tell you was that I saw him briefly talking to a girl in the line at the grocery store and they were smiling at each other, but that was really all that I saw. Truth is the combination of knowledge and understanding. When you have both, great visions can come alive in your life. Add this to character and your faith will continue to be built.

Recently, I read a book where the author shared a story about Henry Ford, who grew up in an era where having a car was only for rich people. Yet, if you look around today, cars are everywhere. They are simple, reliable and affordable, and this can be credited to Mr. Ford's inventions. While he didn't invent the first car, he did learn from those who did. He studied the blue prints and learned that the cars were outstanding. They were actually quite perfect at that time, but only available to those who could afford to buy the car, plus a chauffeur to drive them from place to place. I think it is safe to say that it was not his invention of the car that Mr. Ford should be credited with, but his vision to make the car-making process better.

With much research of the car industry, Mr. Ford noticed that people were making cars by hand, which was a slow and unproductive way of doing things. While that way was inexpensive and accepted, he knew that it was time to make a change in his neighborhood. Everyone needed a new fancy, black car, not just the rich. It was time to let go of the horse and buggy. He worked really hard to get knowledge about cars and learned many lessons along the way until one day he finally got a vision. He envisioned the making of cars at a more rapid pace; he envisioned the first assembly line. This vision changed everything about the car making-experience. Before his invention, car-makers were accustomed to walking to a car and working on that one car, with a team of other car-makers, until it was built. Then they would go to work on another car. Now, on the assembly line, machines move the cars to a car-maker who works on certain parts of the car. Then the car moves to the next person (or team) to complete another part. At the end of the line, the car is completely built and inspected. This vision alone sped up the rate in which cars were produced, and led to a very rich and successful life for Mr. Ford.

The message here is: the more you know and understand the greater the impact of your vision. Think about this statement for a second, "The lightening speed of the motorcycle stripped the poor little tree of his leaves." What was your vision? What did you see? Was it the fast bike or the naked tree? Whatever your vision was, you received it because of what you knew. If you have never seen a fast bike or a naked tree, it would be hard to put together a picture in your mind.

Here is a fact: Your – Brain – Is - Amazing! Your ability to take what you know or learn and make a movie out of it that plays in your mind has left many scientists in awe of how great you are.

When you feed your brain with knowledge, the visions you receive can be groundbreaking, especially when you add understanding. You are bound to reach places you have never dreamed to go. Your visions can and will push you forward in life. There is no way you can stay in the darkness and shadows of the world once you get enough knowledge to bring you out.

Activate Your Power...

Give yourself permission to dream again. Get knowledge about those dreams. Try to understand what you have learned, and watch your vision grow and become clearer. The difference between dreams and visions is that you dream while you are asleep, and you get visions while you are awake. You have dreams that are waiting in the dark for you to activate them with knowledge. The result will be groundbreaking visions that will shed light on your situation and change your life for the better.

Reflect on Your Power:

Don't you dream anymore?

Write one of your dreams here and what information you might need to help you get there.

Ex: I dream to one day be a best-selling author. In order to reach this dream, I would need to know how to write a good book, how to publish and how other best-selling authors made it on the list.

_____

_____

_____

_____

_____

_____

Nuggets to Remember:

1. Without any effort at all, you are likely to learn something new every day.

2. Knowledge sheds light and opens your mind to things you never thought possible.

3. Truth = Knowledge + Understanding. Be sure to get both knowledge and understanding because the truth will set you free to see life differently.

4. **YOUR BRAIN IS AMAZING!**

"An idle mind is the devil's workshop." – Grandma Boot
Give your brain something to do!

Power #3: Discipline

"Grow into Greatness"

Arbor Day is a national holiday that is celebrated around the world to encourage people to plant trees and save the environment. As part of this movement, some organizations and local governments give people trees to plant in their neighborhoods. These trees are grown in a nursery for a little while before being released for planting. This allows the tree to mature some before planting it in the ground. Once planted, the owner may take some string, tie it to the tree and stake it in the ground as an anchor. This process provides support to the small tree in its infancy state to ensure that it grows in alignment, not slanted or twisted, but straight up. Without this support early in the growth phase, trees grow crooked and leaning. Often times, these trees are unable to withstand the storms.

Your ideas are the exact same way, when they are starting to grow; they need support and accountability. Your mind needs boundaries. Once you have broken ground in your understanding the visions start to come, your thoughts become vulnerable to your past thoughts, actions and ideals. Fear becomes a factor, and doubt can easily become your downfall. Moving forward with your vision will take intense discipline and self-control. For the tree, the string and wood may look uncomfortable and purposeless, but it is the necessary boundary that is set up to help the tree learn to have control over itself. What necessary boundaries have you set in place so that you can grow properly?

Forty to fifty percent of what we learn to do as humans is learned by habit – by the things we have learned to do on a regular basis. So, half of the things we actually get done have nothing to do with what we learned but everything to do with what we do, practice and act on in some manner by force of habit. This leads me to believe that when reading becomes a habit, not just something that we do because we are told; we will begin to do it more. This is where discipline makes the difference. You are to take what you have learned to do and what you know is right and turn it into a habit. Discipline is the control that is gained by maintaining good habits and releasing bad ones.

I remember when my daughter started running track. After being around other runners, she learned techniques to make her a better. She learned to eat healthier foods and stop drinking sodas, because that's what she observed from the winning runners. She believed that her team could win, and so she had to practice discipline in those areas in order to succeed. She reminded me that, "You are the only person who can control your habits, and although you are just one person, there are people in your life who are depending on you." Your team (family, friends, etc.) are depending on you to win.

So, why are habits so important? A habit is the part of your character that marks what you do repeatedly. When you are learning to be disciplined in a certain area, you must be willing to change some of your own habits. There's an interesting point: <u>habits can be changed</u>. They change in your mind first, then your heart and then your actions. For instance, have you ever run a marathon? Yeah, me either, but that does not mean I don't understand the insane amount of discipline it takes to prepare and show up for the race, which is perhaps the reason why I've never run one. People who run marathons know that it takes faith to believe that one can complete such an immense task. What makes the difference, what determines those who finish from those who don't, is how or if he or she builds upon their faith before the run begins. So, the marathon runner must be fully aware and have understanding of which habits must be changed or formed in order to succeed.

A well-known philanthropist once said that "In order to succeed, your desire for success should be greater than your *fear* of failure." To succeed at this race, the runner must have this type of desire: Faith over Failure. When you build upon your faith by adding the seven powers, fear is cancelled out. The runner who takes the time to build will have power over fear. By faith, the runner must know, without a shadow of doubt, that they can complete the race. In character, they will know what they are capable of doing and will value the completion of the race more than anything. With knowledge, a good runner will know the distance of the run and understand how long it should take him to complete it. Through discipline, he understands the purpose, and therefore put every effort he has into maintaining habits that could help him succeed, and getting rid of habits that could cause him to lose. He grows as a runner, and he disciplines himself for greatness.

If we lived a life that builds upon our faith, we do not live with concern of when or where it will end. It is not as if we would know the time or the place where our lives will end. We, merely, live each day in preparation, running our very own marathon, and growing to get closer to our victories.

Activate Your Power...
It is imperative that you take control of your thoughts by renewing your mind every day. Make an effort to read the word of God, walk by faith, and continue to build upon it with the power of discipline. Lastly, identify some habits that you need to change in order to succeed in life and make those changes.

Your Greatness is depending on your Discipline.

Reflect on your Power:
We all have some habits that we need to change. For me, it is being a couch potato. I need to form a new habit of exercising each day for at least 30 minutes.
What are some habits that you need to change?
List them here:

_____

_____

_____

_____

_____

_____

Nuggets to Remember:

1. Live a life of discipline.

2. You are the only person who can control your habits.

3. Habit = the part of your character that marks what you do repeatedly. These things determine your success.

4. About one-half of the things we do are done because of habits we have formed, so make sure your habits support the things you want to accomplish in life.

Power #4: Perseverance

"Be Strong"

The Oak Tree, a poem by Johnny Ray Ryder Jr., reads:

"A mighty wind blew night and day
It stole the Oak Tree's leaves away
Then snapped its boughs and pulled its bark
Until the Oak was tired and stark

But still the Oak Tree held its ground
While other trees fell all around
The weary wind gave up and spoke.
How can you still be standing Oak?

The Oak Tree said,
I know that you can break each branch of mine in two
Carry every leaf away
Shake my limbs and make me sway.

But I have roots stretched in the earth
Growing stronger since my birth
You'll never touch them, for you see
They are the deepest part of me.

Until today, I wasn't sure
Of just how much I could endure.
But now I've found, with thanks to you

I'm stronger than I ever knew."

Ryder portrays the oak tree as an epitome of perseverance. If you were to add perseverance with what you believe, who you are, what you know, and how much you've grown, I'm sure what you will get is something truly remarkable. Something as remarkable as a sixty-foot standing Oak Tree with great big branches that bulge above the top, twice as wide as the tree's trunk is long. Research has shown that even after an oak tree has died at age 40, it continues to stand and produce fruit until the tender age of 200 or more. Regardless of the storm or the stressful weight of hundreds of pounds of branches and blooms, the Oak Tree still reminds us that strength prevails. I bet if you learned how to do what the Oak Tree does, you, too, could stand tall and strong. I wonder how successful you could be if you did like the oak tree: moved forward with perseverance.

Perseverance is the spiritual staying power that will die before it gives in. It is a relentless pursuit! Having the patience to passionately wait while doing what is right and not giving in to temptation or trial.

This is the definition of perseverance and one of our hardest powers to develop. Few people like to wait. We live in a world where things are expected right here and right now. Waiting seems to be a thing of the past. We have microwaves, super fast cars and fifteen checkout lines at the local supermarket because no one wants to wait. We are all in such a hurry. It's a shame.

There are some things that cannot be rushed such as developing muscle. Any fitness guru will tell you that building muscle and developing strength does not happen overnight. This process takes both time and effort. It takes perseverance. When you have a fitness goal or have decided that you really want to lose weight, you must push towards your goal passionately. You cannot be relaxed in your actions, exercising three times one week and then none the next, and expect to build muscle. It does not work that way. The fulfillment of your goals will take time - time that you must sacrifice. I know you have been told that there is only 24 hours in a day or there is just not enough time, but when you use each of the hours you have each day to your advantage amazing things can happen. When you are willing to do what's in your heart regardless of any opposition, time becomes a non-factor because perseverance also takes effort. It is so important that you learn to plan your work and work your plan.

Lately, I have been watching the UFC fights on TV with my husband. What I love about watching it is the preparation these men and women go through physically, mentally and spiritually to put them in a position to choose pain. Once they enter the ring for a match, pain is no longer just a thought, it is now a reality. These people have chosen pain as a career. They spend every day taking hits and throwing them back, working on their fancy footwork, ultimately learning how to get out of tight situations.

It is admirable to see how some of them just refuse to "tap out" or give in to the pain which lasts round after round. However, others of them get into the first tight spot and immediately give up or "tap out." Face it; life will be filled with painful hits of something, whether it is losing a loved one, paying bills or, perhaps, poor performance at work or school. Some of us may even be facing diagnosis of a disease. We know that with faith all things are possible. The Bible teaches us that. What we tend to forget is that with perseverance we make the impossible possible for us. The Bible also teaches that without work, or taking some action, faith is not alive. In essence, we must actively pursue our passions in order to raise our faith. Keep these points in mind during your next fight:

When life hits you with a jab, hit it back.

If life says no, you say, "No thanks," and look for the next opportunity. All the time remembering that, God has the final say-so.

When life says you can't, you say, "I can and I will."

There is much to learn about spiritual staying power from studying the oak tree. As mentioned in the poem, the roots of the oak tree are a significant part of its strength. The roots of the tree can mirror its branches and stretch as far below ground as its branches do above, giving it both balance and symmetry. To persevere, we must understand that we have this same ability to create balance and symmetry in our lives and to stand against all odds. The depths of who you are, what is found in your roots, is more than capable of making it through whatever tests life throws your way.

The humble reality of knowing that I can, at any point, be amongst the poor, the brokenhearted, the captive, the prisoners, or the mourners reminds me that no one is exempt from the painful reality of life. In the Bible, the prophet Isaiah gives us hope that God will restore healing, freedom, comfort, care and joy. Furthermore, as we are restored, God will call us *Oaks of Righteousness.* With all that we have just learned of the mighty oak tree, I am glad that God can restore me back to something of such strength and grace. It brings me joy to know that God himself has renamed me an *Oak of Righteousness* and not after my past pains and sins. Know that he has done the same for you.

Activate Your Powers

Here is your chance to be renamed. Remind yourself often that you are an Oak of Righteousness. You can stand against all odds. Your roots run deep, and you have the ability to change lives. If you learn to push through your circumstances, you will discover (just like the Mighty Oak Tree) that you are stronger than you ever knew.

Reflect on Your Power...

Have you ever faced something in life that was hard? I mean it was super hard!
Reflect on that moment and record it here. Then write one thing you did to make it through that moment.

_____

_____

_____

_____

_____

_____

_____

Nuggets to Remember:

1. The oak tree is an epitome of perseverance; take notes from it.

2. Passionately, push towards your goals.

3. Be willing to do what is in your heart, regardless of opposition.

4. When you add perseverance to self-discipline, the impossible becomes possible for you.

Power #5: Godliness

"My Worship is For Real"

Godliness defined:

(1) the power that grows from within that connects who I am with what I was put here to do;

(2) the power that connects the building of my faith through character, knowledge, self-control, and perseverance so that I can reach many people through kindness and love;

(3) a power that is only developed once I have conformed to God's ways and wishes to fulfill my purpose in the earth

The power that we have in godliness connects who we are on the inside with the purpose we are to fulfill on the outside. Without this power we will have the tendency to be either self-righteous with little care for others or over-caring with little concern for self. If we only focus on the four powers that we have already activated, we will live our lives being our own super heroes. There is no doubt that we will be happy and possibly rich, but is that all we want out of life? Please don't tell me that you have dulled your life's meaning down to temporary feelings and the inconsistency of money. There is more to life than this.

Picture for a moment the Mighty Oak Tree, and think about its structure. Surely, it wanted to be happy and to produce lots of fruit, so here is what it did. The seed of the tree was planted, and the roots grew underground where they could not be seen. The trunk sprouted from the ground and then grew slowly as to not rush the process of internal growth. Then, one day, it grew branches and made a connection with the world outside of itself. The branches on top of the tree mirrored the roots that had grown beneath, and the oak tree found a balance between what was inside (unseen) and what it could offer to the world (the seen), Through its branches, leaves and acorns the oak tree continues to provide shade from the sun, healing for our wounds, and food for the animals.

There's a growth process in the human spirit that looks much like the oak tree and when fully developed can provide some of the same benefits, including joy and wealth. When we are building our faith to the seventh power, from faith to love, the spiritual part of us will grow from seeds that are planted through the Word of God. When very little focus is put on the Word of God the spiritual part of us will still grow, but not the way God intended. Instead, the spirit will grow from seeds that are planted from the world, from evil influences, and from Satan. I suggest we all read the Word of God more often so that the next steps of our growth cycle can lead to something good. Remember, what you grow on the inside will be what you produce on the outside.

In our hearts, the seeds that we plant will help to establish our values, beliefs and virtue. If these things are good and focused on God, we will get to know God and understand that He does exist and that he does care. Then, our spirit can break through the hard shells of our hearts that have been formed by life's experiences. As we continue to experience life, God helps us through wisdom to follow his rules and ways, and when we are obedient, God will add power, joy, and wealth to our lives.

I'm grateful for the power of godliness. It serves such a key function in my life: BALANCE. I know so many people who are searching this world for balance in their homes and career; women who are trying to balance the duties of being a wife, a mother, a coworker and friend; a son or daughter who is balancing "life on the edge" at school and a "Christian" life at home. The truth of this power has nothing to do with a title or location. It has everything to do with the balance between who you are and what you were created to do.

So, who are you?

A child of God?

The child of a ruler who is almighty, all-powerful and all-knowing?

Are you created in the image of God?

Yes! Yes, you are!

God created the entire world in seven days. He is all things imaginable and unimaginable. He designed each one of us perfect in his sight, infused us with powers and strength so that we may live with purpose. He then sent us to earth as representatives of Him. You are the walking, talking, tangible depiction of God on the earth. What you have been sent here to do with those abilities is between you and God, but whatever it is, don't hesitate to get started. Going after your purpose will bring balance to your internal growth.

Activate Your Power

Stop living a lopsided life - one without balance. Build upon your perseverance with godliness. Know, without a shadow of doubt, that everything you have gone through up to this point has made you who you are and is waiting for you to grab hold of the promises of God, through his Word, to live in your purpose. Remind yourself daily of who you are in Christ.

Reflect on Your Power...

What do you think you were put on earth to do? Why do you think God put you here?

_____

_____

_____

_____

_____

_____

Nuggets to Remember:

1. Your power of godliness can only be developed once you have conformed to God's ways.

2. Godliness helps us to live a balanced life.

3. What you grow on the inside (in your heart) will reflect what you produce on the outside (in your life).

4. You are a child of God!

Power #6: Kindness
"Giving on Purpose"

Amongst today's hot Christian topics is that of **PURPOSE**. Every well-known pastor or motivational speaker has written a book on finding your purpose trying to convince me that 'I am not an accident, and that everyone has a purpose. Each of their writings has proven the popularity of the topic as they continuously top the charts of bestseller lists around the world.

My question to you is this: "Did you really need for someone to write it in a book?"

I'll be the first to admit, "I needed those books." I wanted someone else to tell me that I have a purpose in this world. I needed to hear (or read) that I was designed to do something purposeful with my life. I thought about it often, but I needed to hear it again. I wanted to feel it in my heart, like the superheroes I watch in the movies.

Over the past 10 years I have watched a lot of superhero movies thanks to a husband who is determined to make me watch them all. One thing I have noticed in those movies is how many of our popular superheroes were sent to earth to serve. They were sent from their "home" to fulfill a certain purpose. Then, it dawned on me, "So were we!" God sent you and me here for a purpose.

I once heard someone say, "Take your right hand and put it on the left side of your chest. If you feel a heartbeat, then you have a purpose."

What is that purpose? I truly believe that "Only God knows." I have searched and searched for purpose in my life and this is what I know for sure. I am to take care of what God has given me (body, life, family, friends, stuff, job, etc.). I am to be an ambassador sent from heaven, so that other people will believe in God.

My next question was, "Exactly how am I supposed to be an ambassador? How can I be an ambassador for God?"

Somewhere in the midst of watching one of the superhero movies I had an 'Ah Ha' moment, "When I am kind to others, I am fulfilling my purpose." I've learned that the number one power of all heroes is kindness. To be a true ambassador of heaven, we must show other people about God through kindness.

Oxford Dictionary defines purpose as 'the reason for which something is done or created.' You were created to do many things, but I believe that the core of God's motive for creating us was kindness. Think about it; with the same heartbeat we use to find purpose, we also use to measure a person's level of kindness. In America, we often describe people who are unfriendly and inconsiderate as being "heartless" or "mean." We search in every person for a certain level of generosity, and in each of us, there's a longing to know that someone else cares.

If your heartbeat was measured by your level of kindness, would you be pleased with the results? Would God?

If an angel appeared before you with a measurement tool like a pedometer that counts steps to measure your level of kindness would his report to God be good or would it read, "This person does not care"? Would it imply that you are heartless? Would the test results prove that you are not kind at all?

How would you rate your own level of kindness? Do you really care? Do you care for others? Do you care for people even when they cannot provide any immediate benefit to your life? Do you care for strangers? Widows? The homeless or poor?

On a scale of 1-10, how kind are you if 10 indicate that you are extremely kind and giving and 1 means that you are not? I believe that there is one thing that keeps us from recognizing our purpose. It is our own selfish desires to discover what that purpose is and what it can do for us, but we must remember that with every purpose there is intent. I have learned that I do have a purpose, and it is made clear with every act of intentional kindness. Therefore, I must be willing to rate my heart towards others and be willing to serve. It is part of my purpose.

Probably, the kindest people I know are teachers. Teachers tend to be kind people. In my book, their level of kindness would rate about an 8 or 9. I have met many teachers who are able to show kindness to a room of about 25 kids they do not know. They clean the scars of these children when parents are not around. They wipe the tears of the child with a defeated heart. They rebuild the deferred dreams in hopeless youth. Teachers are showing kindness in ways that are unimaginable to many of us. They give of themselves, on purpose; whether paid or unpaid.

Teachers give on purpose and have, for me, been an awesome example of how each of us should live our lives every day.

The first day of school each year, I make it a point to walk through the school with my youngest child. I look at the little ones as they journey to class, smiling at the school's staff who stand at their room doors with gleaming smiles, ready to meet their new students. Neither of us knows what to expect, and my child's grip usually gets tighter and tighter as each teacher passes by - so does my anxiety. Before long, with my child holding tightly to my hand, we enter the classroom and are greeted by the voice of someone, usually a female, of whom we hope, has found her purpose. We can't say that we will ever know if she has, but we can at least pray that she is kind.

I truly hope that on the way to fulfilling your purpose that you remember the people you meet along the way. Help those you can. Pray for those you can't. But never, not even for a moment, think that you were given a purpose that would only benefit you. Your life and its amazing design longs to give to others the respect and care that they need.

Activate Your Power

Through prayer, ask God to search your heart, to measure your level of kindness. Kindness is a verb and should be acted upon with every chance we get. Ask yourself daily, "Do I care enough about the world I live in and the people I meet to make a difference?" If your answer is "Yes," start today by giving on purpose, and let this fuel your passion.

Reflect on Your Power...

What did you do today to show kindness? How did it make you feel?

_____

_____

_____

_____

_____

Nuggets to Remember:

1. Everyone has a purpose.
2. When you are kind to others, you are fulfilling your purpose and making it clearer.
3. The number one power of superheroes is kindness.
4. Rate your heart towards others and be willing to serve those around you.

Power #7: Love
Love without Limits

November 26th marks the date. Every year on this day I dust off my old Christmas CDs and fill the house with tunes by the Jackson Five, the Temptations, Alvin and the Chipmunks, and many others. Amongst my favorite Christmas carol is the popular song, "Give Love on Christmas Day." I don't care who sings it. I just want to hear it. It seems like every artist from here to England has recorded a version of this song. If you recall, the Lyrics go like this:

> "People making lists
> Hiding special gifts
> Taking time to be kind to one and all
> It's that time of year
> When good friends are dear
> And you wish you could give more
> Than just presents from a store
>
> Why don't you give love on Christmas day?
> Oh, even the man who has everything
> Would be so happy if you would bring
> Him love on Christmas day.
> No greater gift is there than love…"

In every essence of the word, love is great. It's even greater when it is added to kindness. It is the seventh power that we use to build upon our faith. Love seals the deal. If you are a good, wholesome person with all of the knowledge in the world and no love in your heart, you are still incomplete. Love is more than who you are, it is what you do. Love is an action. In 1 Corinthians 13, we are reminded that love perseveres. I believe that it is because of love that we don't give up and that we learn self-discipline. Through love we desire to be a better person for the people we love. This fixation, we call love, when acted on in worship towards God, causes us to worship Him and to be kind to those around us.

Love is number seven in our faith-building process. The number seven has a traditional meaning of completeness and perfection. When we share our love with the world, we add the final touches to our faith because love is the ultimate demonstration of faith at work.

It is by faith that we believe for greatness, but it is by building upon our faith that we grow in greatness. By showing love and kindness to others, we demonstrate our greatness. We share with the world the powers that have grown inside of us through our talents and our gifts.

Speaking of gifts, did you know that some people communicate through gift giving and receiving? "For some people, what makes them feel most loved is receiving a gift," according to the author of "The Five Love Languages," Gary D. Chapman. This concept has brought timeless insight into the way people communicate love. Gift giving is only one way to communicate love, but for many of us it is a tangible way to show the people around us just how much we love them. Whether it is diamonds and pearls, cars, televisions and electronics, money and cards, pictures and other things we value, the sharing of gifts has been a universal symbol of love. Think about it, when is the last time you spent money on someone you did not love?

Up to this point in life, you have probably seen gifts as the receipt or sharing of something tangible, but not all gifts are provided by money. Some gifts are given through time, talent and other resources (like food). Whether it is tangible (something you can touch), spiritual (a special ability given to you from God), or physical (a service completed), it only needs to be given with love.

The Christmas song in the beginning of this chapter shared one of the greatest principles of love that we often forget: Love is the greatest gift we can ever give. Sometimes gifts are not about how much money you can spend but how much love you can expend. Every gift you give should be overflowing with love so that the person receiving it can feel your heart for them through what you have given. Even the person who has everything still needs to feel a love that money cannot buy.

As a person whose love language is gifts, I love, love, love to receive and to give them. I used to recognize gifts as those tangible things that I can hold, play with, wear, or eat. Though, what I have learned about this language is that love can be communicated through other gifts, such as a kind word, a ride home, a prayer or a good joke. They all have made me feel loved and in turn, inspired me to give love to someone else.

This is the purpose of love and the reason it is the last power to be added to our faith. Love is received so that it may be given in faith to someone else, in hopes that they will keep it going. Just like faith has the energy to produce great things, so does love. When love is shared, here is what happens: a piece of fruit drops from your tree. You still have lots of other love fruits on your tree, but you just shared one with the world.

As the "Oak of Righteousness," you have lots of acorns (or love fruit) to share. As you drop them, animals or people come by and pick them up. It provides nourishment to them. It makes them smile. It is something that they can then share with their family and friends. Love works the same way. When you share it with those around you through kindness, godliness, knowledge, or by just being you, you give them joy and something that they can share with others.

I challenge you to give gifts every day. Share your smile and kind words. Share your resources with those in need. Share your time and talents to help others. We know that even the smallest gift can touch someone's heart. It shows your gratitude. It communicates gratefulness. Sharing your gifts with others gives a testimony of God's goodness on the earth. Through love we express this goodness and complete the building process of our faith.

The bible says that love is one of the fruits of the spirit and that against these fruit, there is no law. Whether it is through a girlfriend/boyfriend or husband/wife relationship, love is love. Parents love their kids. Pet-lovers love their animals. I love you. No matter the relationship, love is still love. So, why do we insist on making love what we want it to be or do what we want it to do?

We can only share the love that we have. When it is received by the next person it is planted as a seed of faith in his/her heart and the building process begins in them. We cannot control when or if they will show love to someone else. We can only hope they will.

As the final power of our faith, love perfects our race. It connects us to resources beyond our limits. Love, when it is added as the final power, will take you further than your character, beyond all knowledge, and through challenging perseverance. It will humble you in self-discipline and shower you in God's grace. Love is expressed in kindness. It leaves our heart in small portions, so that faith can be perfected. Love has no limits on who it will reach or how far it will stretch. If we set our faith and build upon it, love will help someone else do the same.

Activate Your Powers

Don't wait for the holidays and special occasions to show people love. Strangers, outcasts, widows, children, family members, they all need your love. Be patient. Be kind. Do not be jealous, full of yourself, or conceited. Don't be easily angered or continuously remind people of their wrongs. Rejoice in the truth! Be someone's protector. Be trustworthy. Be hopeful. And remember, that love NEVER fails. Take the limits off... love freely. (I Corinthians 13:4-8)

Reflect on Your Power...

Now that you know that love is a super power, how will you use it to change your world?

_____

_____

_____

_____

_____

_____

Nuggets to Remember:

1. Love is the greatest gift we can ever give.

2. Love is the ultimate demonstration of faith at work.

3. Gifts come in three forms: tangible (something you can touch), spiritual (a special ability given to you from God), or physical (a service completed).

4. When love is shared, a piece of fruit drops from your tree. Someone else picks it up, enjoys it, and shares it with others.

Powers Activated

As a child, I remember watching a cartoon named "Captain Planet." There were many people in the group, but they each harnessed their own power. One was able to control water and another one wind. When they put their powers together, they were able to change the world. I wished for superpowers and remember thinking, "Maybe if I could fly I would find a happier home." Or, "What if I could run really fast? Then, it wouldn't take as long to get my chores done." I never did get those superpowers and I probably never will.

Did you know that we have powers that are greater than speed and flight? These powers are working inside of you right now. If you activate them and continue to let them grow in your life you will find that life is actually happy right where you are and that running fast only makes you miss the great things that are going on around you.

It is my earnest belief that with the activation of each of your powers, your faith is being built higher and higher. I also believe that you are now well equipped with the understanding of eight very valuable principles that should be added to your life. I hope that you have considered what life could be like if you could build your faith.

If not, let's think about it. "What would your life be like if you seriously and wholeheartedly lived a life that continuously builds upon your faith?"

The Bible says in Hebrew 11:6 that without faith it is impossible to please God (ASV) and when God is pleased he gives us supernatural strength (Nehemiah 8:10).

Have you ever set your heart on something, started moving towards the achievement of a goal only to quit along the way? It is not until you have gone after something of value that you fully understand just how important these powers are to your life. I dare you to Dream Big and strive for abundance!

Here's a tip so that you do not get discouraged: Define your own success. Don't give that responsibility to the world and to hip hop videos. What does abundance look like for you? For some people, abundance has been minimized to big houses and fancy cars. But, the true meaning of abundance is "plentifulness of the good things of life." Take a moment and ask yourself, "What are my good things in life and do I have plenty of it?" Some of my good things include family, friends, good health, a clear mind, chocolate and great working taste buds (I told you I like to eat).

Through faith in God, the Bible promises each of us an abundant life. It promises that we can have the good things and that we can have lots of it. However, there are some factors we must consider. There are some powers we must activate in order to receive this abundance. The first of these powers is to believe. Try to remember that your faith is always your first and most dominant power to bringing good things into your life, but like they say in the movies, "With great power comes great responsibility." So, here are some questions to consider about your new found power.

1) Are you doing things in your life that builds faith or are you sitting and waiting for something to happen?

2) Are you hoping for greatness or are you thinking that greatness is not something that will happen for you?

3) Are you dreaming big? Do you have a vision that is groundbreaking and earth-shattering?

4) Are you disciplined enough to go after the greatness you want?

5) What are you doing repeatedly in your everyday life that will help you?

6) Are you standing like the mighty Oak Tree or are you whimpering at every challenge you face?

7) Are you worshipping God for real or are you playing?

8) Are you giving on purpose everyday or only at Christmas time?

9) Do you recognize that you have time, talent, and resources that were given to you as a gift that you must share with the world?

10) Do you love without limits, unconditionally, or does your love always come with some sort of stipulation (not right now, I would love you if...)?

I would like to warn you that "Change is not easy." In fact, for many people change is extremely difficult. However, that does not mean it shouldn't be done. If we want to have a life that is full of "good things," we must first believe and then we must build. Faith is the foundation of all that we do and the most important factor in our relationship with God. But, as a child of God, that is not enough for you. You want plenty of the good things.

So, just for you, God gave seven extra powers that will make you super! These powers set you above the rest and must grow in your life every day. They will bring reward and all of the good things that your heart desires.

Remember, in all things, consider these powers:

Power 1: Character

Harness your greatness by building your character and recognizing what you value most about life.

Power 2: Knowledge

Learn something new and allow yourself to dream again.

Power 3: Self-Control

Be disciplined in going after your "good things". Self control is your key to winning.

Power 4: Perseverance

Challenges will come and go, but you must stand strong and keep believing.

Power 5: Godliness

Living in godliness is more than super-holy-religiosity. It is about connections and relationships with the Lord and with people around you.

Power 6: Kindness

Re-treasure the gift giving process and use your gifts to fulfill your purpose. Be kind to one and all.

Power 7:

Love is lawless. It cannot be controlled by magic or selfish desires. Take the limits off of your love, and allow it to express itself in your everyday life.

Like muscles, these powers must be strengthened. Faith is strengthened through prayer, praise, and preparation for living a life that is holy before God. How do you think we can strengthen the seven powers God has given us to raise our faith? It would not be the right thing to do if we lived our life with these awesome gifts, but did nothing to keep them up. If you received a new car today, what would you do to keep it up? What if you received a $100? Would you spend it all at once or make plans for it? You have been granted these amazing super powers as a gift from God. Do not hoard them or waste them. It is up to you to build upon them and allow them to grow in your life.

Reflect on Your Activated Powers...
What have you done today to strengthen your powers of character, knowledge, discipline, perseverance, godliness, kindness, and love?

_____

_____

_____

_____

Nuggets to Remember:

1. Connect with the powers within you to do great things.

2. Life is happy, right where you are.

3. Dream big and strive for abundance (a life full of good things).

4. We must build upon our faith in order to receive the abundant life that God has promised us.

Always be mindful of scripture when you are building your faith. **Romans 10:17 (NIV)** of the bible reads, "…Faith comes by hearing the message, and the message is heard through the word about Christ." Read these scriptures and allow them minister to your heart.

Matthew 17:20 (MSG) – "Because you're not yet taking God seriously," said Jesus. "The simple truth is that if you had a mere kernel of faith, a poppy seed, say, you would tell this mountain, 'Move!' and it would move. There is nothing you wouldn't be able to tackle."

2 Peter 1:8 (MSG) – With these qualities active and growing in your lives, no grass will grow under your feet, no day will pass without its reward as you mature in your experience of our Master Jesus.

2 Peter 1:5-7 (MSG) – So don't lose a minute in building what you've been given, complementing your basic faith with good character, spiritual understanding, alert discipline, passionate patience, revert wonder, warm friendliness, and generous love, each dimension fitting into and developing the others.

James 2:20 (MSG) – Do I hear you professing to believe in the one and only God, but then observe you complacently sitting back as if you had done something wonderful? That's just great. Demons do that, but what good does it do them? Use your head! Do not suppose for a minute that you can cut faith and works in two and not end up with a corpse on your hands?

Proverbs 4:7 (KJV) – Wisdom is the principal thing; therefore get wisdom: and with all thy getting get understanding.

Mark 9:23 (MSG) – Jesus said, "If? There are no 'ifs' among believers. Anything can happen."

Isaiah 61:1-7 (MSG) – The Spirit of God, the Master, is on me because God anointed me.

He sent me to preach good news to the poor, heal the heartbroken, announce freedom to all captive, and pardon all prisoners.

God sent me to announce the year of his grace – a celebration of God's destruction of our enemies – and to comfort all who mourn. To care for the needs of all who mourn in Zion, give them bouquets of roses instead of ashes, Messages of joy instead of news of doom, a praising heart instead of a languid spirit. Rename them "Oaks of Righteousness" planted by God to display his glory.

They'll rebuild the ruins; raise a new city out of the wreckage. They'll start over on the ruined city, take the rubble left behind and make it new. You'll hire outsiders to herd your flock and foreigners to work your fields…

1 Corinthians 13:3-8 (MSG) – If I give everything I own to the poor and even go to the stake to be burned as a martyr, but I don't love, I've gotten nowhere. So, no matter what I say, what I believe, and what I do, I'm bankrupt without love.

Love never gives up.
Love cares more for others than for self.
Love doesn't want what it doesn't have.
Love doesn't strut,
Doesn't have a swelled head,
Doesn't force itself on others,
Isn't always "me first,"
Doesn't fly off the handle,
Doesn't keep score of the sins of others,
Doesn't revel when others grovel,
Takes pleasure in the flowering of the truth,
Puts up with anything,
Trusts God always,
Always looks for the best,
Never looks back,
But keeps going to the end,
Love never dies.

Galatians 5: 22-24 – But what happens when we live God's way? He brings gifts into our lives, much the same way that fruit appears in an orchard – things like affection for others, exuberance about life, serenity. We develop a willingness to stick with things, a sense of compassion in the heart, and a conviction that a basic holiness permeates things and people. We find ourselves involved in loyal commitments, not needing to force our way in life, able to marshal and direct our energies wisely. Legalism is helpless in bringing this about; it only gets in the way. Among those who belong to Christ, everything connected with getting our own way and mindlessly responding to what everyone else calls necessities is killed off for good – crucified.

Hebrews 11: 6 – It's impossible to please God apart from faith. And why? Because anyone who wants to approach God must believe both that he exists and that he cares enough to respond to those who seek him.

Nehemiah 8:10 – He continued, "Go home and prepare a feast, holiday food and drink; and share it with those who don't have anything: This day is holy to God. Don't feel bad. The joy of God is your strength.

Message from the Author

It has been my dream since youth that you would read my book. I wanted to give up. I knew for myself that faith took work. But, God saw different. So, I pray that by activating the powers laid out in this book, you are able to win in life.

It is my purpose to give of the gifts that God has given to me. Thank you for allowing me to share the gift of writing with you. May it be a message of hope that will motivate you and your family to achieve the greatness you desire. I have faith that through a relationship with God, you will achieve the impossible. You got this. Now, Go, Do, Believe, and Achieve. Live your life at the 7th power, invest in yourself, and raise your faith.

Feel free to communicate with me via email at beopulentbydesign@gmail.com.

www.ingramcontent.com/pod-product-compliance
Lightning Source LLC
Chambersburg PA
CBHW060428050426
42449CB00009B/2187